**UNCAP YOUR LIFE**
**YOU SHALL HAVE WHAT YOU SAY!**

# TABLE OF CONTENTS

# UNCAP YOUR LIFE
## by Apostle Octavia Standley

I'm writing this guide or reference book due to a revelation I received from the Holy Spirit, I will discuss that a little later in this book.

This guide or book is designed to be a *quick pick me up* in hard times.

I am excited about the things I'm going to share with you as I know that it will change your life forever!

The title of my book is UNCAP YOUR LIFE (You shall have what you say.) To **uncap** something means to take the limits off, conversely to cap something or to put a cap on something as defined by *FreeDictionary.com* is to put a **limit** on something. An example of this is to say, "We need to put a cap or a limit" on our spending.

Putting a "cap" on something is also defined as to set an **"upper limit"** on something (i.e. a budget).

If you put a "cap" on something you are figuratively and literally (in the spirit) setting a limit on yourself. You have determined that you can only go so high; you can't get beyond this point!

Many of you have unknowingly put a "cap" on your life! You're wondering why your life is the way it is, why your finances are the way they are, why your children won't act right , your marriage or relationships continue to fail despite all of your prayer and now you've "thrown in the towel" and said "I'm done!"

You my friend have put a "cap" on your life!

Using an experience and resulting revelation that actually happened to me; as well as some biblical principles, I will show you how to take the "CAP" off of your life!

## YOU SHALL HAVE WHAT YOU SAY
### Mark 11:23, 24

*For verily I say unto you, that whosoever shall say*
*unto this mountain,*
*Be thou removed, and be thou cast into the sea;*
*and shall not doubt in his heart,*
*but shall believe that those things which he saith*
*shall come to pass;*
*he shall have whatsoever he saith. Therefore I say*
*unto you,*
*What things so ever ye desire, when ye pray,*
*believe that ye receive them,*
*and ye shall have them.*

One day my husband and I were watching a well-known preacher on a popular Christian Broadcasting Station. For a while he was preaching and preaching well I might add, but then suddenly he began to make some declarations **(the formal announcement of the beginning of a state or condition.)** that at first sounded really good but one of those declarations caught the Holy Ghosts' attention.

I'm going to side step just a second as I really need you to take notice of that definition. A declaration ANNOUNCES THE BEGINNING OF a state or condition. You shall have what you say because YOU SAID IT!

One of the declarations he made and had the audience repeat was "This year will be the **best** year of my life!!" with gusto the audience as well as my husband began to repeat the declaration but immediately in my spirit I heard the Holy Ghost say, "DON'T SAY

THAT! "and it wasn't a still small voice either! HE went on to explain "if you do, you'll put a "Cap" on your life and whatever 2016 holds for you, that's the **best** you're gonna get."

WOW......deep huh? It hit me in the stomach like a fist!

I followed the leading of the Holy Ghost and instead of making that declaration; I said "this will be ONE OF MANY of the best years of my life!"
I shared with my husband what the Holy Spirit said and he instantly began to **RENOUNCE, REPENT, REVERSE AND REINVENT** (We'll discuss these later in the book) what he had previously declared.

My husband and I then both begin to renounce, repent, and reverse every previous declaration that we had ever made over the years and starting "reinventing" the way our lives shall be!

Think about it, how many of you have in rote or mechanical repetition stated what a preacher or life coach or even an inspirational speaker said just because what they said sounded good?

Maybe you too have declared this will be the best year of my life!
Be honest, I'm sure everyone reading this has at one time or another. I know I sure have.

Maybe your declaration wasn't what someone else said; maybe you, because of your current situation have declared something like this:

> *it doesn't get any better than this!
> *this is a good as it gets!
> *he/she will never change!
> *I can never keep any money in my account

Or any such idioms (combination of words that have a "figurative meaning")
If you have, and I'm almost certain you have, you my friend have "Capped your Life!"

Let's look at some more biblical principles that relate to our "having what we say" starting with the scriptures surrounding our reference scripture.

In Mark 11 starting with the 11th verse we find Jesus walking up on a fig tree. It had leaves on it so Jesus started looking for fruit. When he didn't see any on the tree (which really represented Israel) he cursed the tree and *SAID* that no one would ever eat from that tree again. When they walked by the fig tree the next day, Peter noted that it had indeed dried up just as *Jesus had spoken.*

Jesus SPOKE A CURSE and the fig tree withered up and died!

Do you realize that same power is in you? When you SPEAK you cause things to happen in the spirit realm. There are NO IDLE WORDS! If you speak it, it will manifest! The sum total of your life right now is a result of the things you have thought and said.

 Now don't get me wrong, you can't just sit on the couch and declare, "I'm going to be a millionaire" but never get off of your behind to do anything! Those are just idle words with no faith! Why do I say with no faith? Because faith will cause you to move on! It will cause you to put a plan into action, a plan that ACCOMPANIED by your words will cause manifestation!

Understand this, you can't think you can speak things that are outside of Gods will or against His commands and think you'll get those! You can't speak and declare by faith that you'll have someone else's husband or wife and think you're going to get them! You can't take someone's life and declare by faith you won't get caught and go to jail! Those things go against His very nature! You can't declare you're going to take over someone's ministry and God never planned for you to walk in that office! He will not give you what He has not ordained! He will however give you what His word has already declared you can have!

Faith in God's word will cause you to act in accordance with His word.
The bible tells us we are the temple of God! It is our job to care for that temple spiritually and physically. You cannot ask God to heal you of diabetes but won't exercise enough discipline and self-control to stop eating snack cakes and drinking soda!

If you are a born again believer, the promises of God are yes and amen in Him! Start speaking what He says you already have access to and cause it to manifest in your life!

One of the problems I find is that many don't realize that when they speak negative words against themselves they are actually speaking **faith filled** words! They believe what they say about themselves and they ACT accordingly! This causes satan to go into action on your behalf and bring what you say into manifestation!

Words have creative force behind them. You're either going to cause God to move on your behalf or you're going to cause the devil to! Your words have life!

Start speaking not what you see but what you desire to see! Stop speaking the circumstance and start speaking the outcome that you want! Once you start speaking those things that be not as though they already are and accompany your words with corresponding actions, you'll begin to live the life you always desired!

I pray that the next few lessons you read will cause you to pause before you declare anything negative out of your mouth.

 Remember, YOU WILL HAVE WHATSOEVER YOU SAY!

**UNCAP YOUR LIFE**
**YOU SHALL HAVE WHAT YOU SAY!**

# DEATH AND LIFE
## Proverbs 18:21

*Death and life are in the power of the tongue:*
*and they that love it shall eat the fruit thereof.*

Did you catch that? You have the power to speak things into existence and I'm not talking "spooky nonsense!"

What this scripture declares is that the good and bad in your life is the RESULT OF WHAT YOURE ALLOWING TO COME OUT OF YOUR MOUTH!

Verse 20 of this same chapter declares, "A man's belly shall be satisfied with the ***fruit of his mouth*** (what he speaks); and with the increase or produce of his lips shall he be filled!

What you say will literally produce in your life! If you are always speaking negative, your life will be filled with negative things! If you speak positive, affirming, faith filled words; your life will produce positive results! Your tongue and the words you speak are more powerful than what many of you realize!

Let's take a look at the tongue.

On the tongue are what we call taste receptors or what is most commonly known as "taste buds." The tastes our tongues are able to distinguish are **sweet, salty, bitter** and **sour.**

What have you been speaking?

Are your words **Sweet** (positive, affirming, full of hope, Love and peace) or are they **Salty** (mean, hateful, full of rejection and anger?)

Are your words **Bitter** (unforgiving, dark, words full of depression and hopelessness) or are they **Sour** (sharp, unpleasant, unfriendly and disrespectful?)

What you allow to roll off of your tongue will truly affect your life! You can be the kind of person that takes lemons (the sour things of life) and make lemonade or you can sit back with a "sour" face sucking on those lemons. The choice is yours!

Remember, your outlook and response (what you say) to a thing will determine the results that you get!

Because we are made in the image and likeness of God, we possess His same creative authority!

God declared, "Let there be and there was!"

So it is with us. If your declaration continues to be "I can't have, I'll never get, I'm always sick, I'm broke, this ALWAYS HAPPENS to me" you're gonna eat that fruit!

Words are seeds that bring forth a HARVEST, that harvest is your current life!

Start speaking (planting seeds) of growth, prosperity, maturity, long life, family unity, marital success and watch your HARVEST come in a BIG WAY!

You'll see progress and movement instead of standstill and stalemate!

SPEAK LIFE and take the "Cap" off of your Harvest!

# UNCAP YOUR LIFE
## YOU SHALL HAVE WHAT YOU SAY!

# CAUGHT IN A TRAP
## Proverbs 6:2

*Thou art snared with the words of thy mouth,*
*Thou art taken with the words of thy mouth.*

Snare: anything serving to **entrap** or **entangle** unawares; trap.

Merriam-Webster defines **snare** as: a device that has a loop (noose) which gets smaller when the end of it is pulled and that is used to catch animals: a kind of trap: a position or situation from which it is difficult to escape.

How many of you have cosigned a loan for a friend? Have you allowed them to use you as a reference when you know they can't keep a job?
How about letting someone stay with you when you know the reason they lost their own place was because they didn't pay their bills and they trashed the place?

Many times in our "nice and kind" hearts we have allowed ourselves to make a pledge with someone or go into agreement with someone knowing deep down in your "knower" you would regret that decision.

You put your own self in a trap! No, I am not saying don't be there for someone you love but I am saying you better know in your heart of hearts that they are good for what you are about to cosign for or for what you're about to enter into agreement with them in.

When you don't consult the Lord and just make decisions like these out of your "nice and kind" heart, IF they default on that loan, or trash that apartment or act a total fool on that job, YOU WILL BE THE ONE THE LOAN SHARK IS LOOKING FOR!

You'll be the one holding the bill, you'll be the one whose phone is blowing up because of bill collectors, and ultimately you'll be the one who can't get your friend you signed the loan for to answer YOUR calls!

And normally when you do catch up with them, THEY HAVE AN ATTITUDE WITH YOU FOR BRINGING THE MATTER TO THEM!!

Your "yes" to cosigning that loan has now put you in a trap! Read the reference scripture again. It says, "thou are *snared* with the words (your yes) of thy mouth, thou art taken (trapped, bound) with the words of thy mouth.

The words that you speak TRAP you whether good or bad. A snare is normally **hidden** or **camouflaged** in an environment, unobservable to the eye. When people come to you asking you to cosign a loan on a house, car or apartment; they don't tell you that they might forfeit on the loan, oh no, they come with a pretty picture about their new job and how much money that they make and how they can always count on you to have their backs! The picture is painted so pretty that you agree to enter into contract with them. The bad part about that is, the only way you'll know a snare is there is when you step INTO IT! Then when you try to pull away its gets tighter and tighter around your neck, leg or arm refusing to let you go! Now you are responsible for their debt! Next time you are called upon to cosign, THINK before you say yes!

On another note, some of us have spoken a thing or believed a thing not knowing that it was a trap set by the enemy to keep you in the same cycles over and over again! Cycles rehearsed by your parents, their parents, their parents before them and their parents before them! Let's take a look at this trap.

In this section I'm going to talk about family!

How many of you have heard things like:
      *You're just like your daddy
      *He wasn't nothing, you ain't gonna be nothing!
      *Everybody has high blood pressure, you're gonna get it too!
      *The women in this family are strong! We don't need a man!
      *The men in this family don't know how to settle down with one good woman!
      *This family is so divided!

Somehow your experiences in life tell you that these things are "true" so you spend your life believing them and speaking them!

You have stepped into your own snare!

The thing about a snare is that you will either have to gnaw your limb off to escape it or someone will have to cut you out! Either way a snare always leaves a mark!

You need to decide if that "mark" will scar you for the rest of your life or if you'll begin to declare (announce the beginning of something new) with that "mark", **THE BUCK STOPS HERE!**

Decide today to walk out of that trap! Make a NEW MARK in life by declaring:

>*I will not be like my dad/mom; I will walk in what God has for me!
>*I will accomplish and fulfill my destiny even if no one else in my family does!
>*I will not be sick but will walk in healing all the days of my life!
>*Even though I am a strong woman, I will submit to my husband!
>*I will be faithful and love my wife!
>*My marriage will be happy and for LIFE despite the numerous divorces in my family!
>*My past will not dictate my future!
>*I can and I will have all that God has ordained for me!

Somebody needs to decree TODAY that the Family Snares have been sprung and it will not trap me!

**UNCAP YOUR LIFE**
**YOU SHALL HAVE WHAT YOU SAY!**

**UNCAP YOUR LIFE
YOU SHALL HAVE WHAT YOU SAY!**

# ZIP YOUR LIPS!
## Proverbs 13:3

*Whoever guards his mouth preserves his life;*
*He who opens wide his lips comes to ruin.*

Another bible version says, "Those who guard their lips preserve their lives, but those who speak rashly will come to ruin!

I'm sure Samson wishes he had of kept his mouth shut on several occasions! Two different women betrayed him all because he opened his lips. First his wife told his secrets to his enemies (she was an enemy too) and he had to pay them, THEN his girlfriend set him up to be captured and tortured and they both had the power to do it because he opened his mouth and spilled his secrets! He allowed their fake tears to break him down and ultimately it cost him his life!

Sometimes it's just best to be quiet!

Emotional outburst can cause you to speak thing rashly, things that in your sound mind you would know better than to speak!

In the heat of the moment many have been guilty of uttering such words as:

> *I hate this job!
> *I want a divorce!
> *I'm so stupid, Fat, or ugly!
> *I will never forgive you!

\*I don't love you!
\*I'm done with this Christian walk!
\*I wish I never had kids!
\*I hate I married you!
\*I wish I had never been born!
\*I wish you would die!

**Devastating words** huh? Have you ever spoken words in anger? Has anyone ever spoken words of anger to you?

How did it feel? How do you think the other person you spoke to in anger felt?

Did you notice how all of those statements started with "I?" that's because those types of statements come from a self-centered place! The focus is always on _you_ and what _you_ want, not on what is best for those on the receiving end of your words!

Oftentimes, it is hard to restore a friendship, marriage, relationship with your children after emotional outburst like that. Even if you remain around each other the strain, hurt, and pain caused by those words will remain.

By not guarding your mouth and speaking rashly and without thought, you have in essence "capped" your relationships.

Proverbs 12:18 says, **"There is that speaketh like the piercings of a sword: but the tongue of the wise is health!"**

Your words can pierce just like a sword, that means it can go straight to the core of a person and cause damage on the inside! When something is pierced, there is a hole created in it; your words can create a hole in someone that sometimes they are not able to overcome.

Unless there is true repentance, a reversal of those words and a recreating of that relationship,

RUIN WILL BE THE RESULT

Think about the bullying suicides that we've all read about. The words of another or others, pierced through that victims soul, cutting to the heart of them and there was no recovery for them.

Proverbs 18:8 "the words of a talebearer *are as wounds*, and they go down into the *innermost parts* of the belly."

There are Facebook post, tweets on Twitter, Snapchat and Instagram postings that have caused many a teenager to take their lives because the words spread about them, whether true or not pierced and wounded them to the very core.

The saying goes "sticks and stones may break my bones but words will never hurt me." let me tell you something, that saying is a lie! Many people have been devastated by the words of others. Some of the things you have done and or facing right now is because of the words of others.

But there is hope in the midst of the "words storm", that hope is Jesus Christ. God will take those things that were meant for your evil and turn them for your good!

When you feel that "storm" raging inside of you and you are ready to let someone have a piece of your mind; remember this:

### *SILENCE IS GOLDEN! LEARN HOW TO ZIP YOUR LIPS!*

# ACCUSED OR ACQUITTED?
## Matthew 12:37

*For by thy words thou shalt be justified,*
*and by thy words thou shalt be condemned.*

In Matthew 12 starting at the 22<sup>nd</sup> verse we find Jesus doing what He came to do, healing the sick, casting out devils and restoring sight, etc....

In Him just being who He is, He was accused of casting out devils by Beelzebub the prince or ruler of the devils! People just be hating!

One thing I love about Jesus though, He set them straight with a quickness! He said to them in verses 25-28 *"every kingdom divided against itself is brought to desolation; and every city or house divided against itself shall not stand: and if satan cast out satan, he is divided against himself; how shall then his kingdom stand? And if I by Beelzebub cast out devils, by whom do your children cast them out? Therefore they shall be your judges. (Ha!! get em Jesus!)*
*Verse 28 But if I cast out devils by the Spirit of God, then the Kingdom of God is come unto you.*

In other words he asked them, "How in the world would the kingdom of darkness stand if it fought against itself? You are accusing me of something and your own children do it so if I'm guilty, so is your offspring!

You know that particular accusation stopped! They knew Jesus WAS KINGDOM; no devil in hell could do what He did!

To be accused is to be charged with or on trial for a crime. *Merriam-Webster* defines it as: a person who has been arrested for or formally charged with a crime: the defendant in a criminal case.

To be *acquitted* according to *(legal-dictionary.thefreedictionary.com)* means the **legal** finding, by judge or jury that an accused person is not guilty of the crime he/she is charged with. It is the legal and formal certification of the innocence of a person who has been charged with a crime

I like the explanation of acquitted or acquittal by *Cornell University* that I found on Google! It said, "An acquittal signifies that a prosecutor failed to prove his or her case beyond a reasonable doubt, *not that a defendant is innocent!*

Jesus was falsely accused AND PROVEN INNOCENT of every charge they ever threw at Him!

Many reading this book have been accused of gossip or slander. Some of you rightfully so, some of you were wrongfully accused and some of you threw a rock and hid your hand, in other words, they didn't catch you but you were still guilty!

1 Peter 4:15 says, "But let none of you suffer as a murderer, or as a thief, or as an evildoer, or as a *busybody* in other men's matters.

I want you to take this time and be honest with yourself (go on, nobody else is looking) if you are guilty of being a busybody, running around and telling EVERYBODYS business, REPENT right now! Ask the Lord to remove that gossiping spirit from you and mean it from your heart. Repentance means you DONT GO BACK TO IT!

You reap what you sow. You can't go around talking about others, revealing private and intimate faults and issues about them and not expect that same thing to come back to you or worse!

Words, like bullets shot from a gun can never be taken back! They keep going until they hit a target! What people don't realize when they gossip about others or slander the names of others is that "bullets also ricochet!" your words may just bounce off of the receiver and come back to haunt you!

Proverbs 6:16-19 says, " These six things doth the Lord *hate*: yea, seven are an abomination unto Him: a proud look, *a lying* tongue, and hands that shed innocent blood, an *heart that deviseth wicked imaginations*, feet that be swift in running to mischief, a *false witness that speaketh lies, and he that soweth discord among brethren."*

God hates tale-bearing, He hates discord amongst the brethren; please understand that doing these things will not only "cap" your life; it will "cap" your potential, "cap" your blessings and put a "cap" on your destiny!

Why do I say that? The bible say in John 8:44 that you are of your father the devil and the lust of your father, ye will do. He was a *liar* from the beginning and abode not in the truth. The bible also says that the devil is the accuser of the brethren!"

so when you are lying, when you are gossiping, when you are slandering and looking for something or someone to talk about, you are operating JUST LIKE THE DEVIL and he ain't getting nothing from the Lord but judgment into eternal damnation!

Do you realize that you will be held accountable for every word that comes out of your mouth?

In court rooms all around the world, many defendants are being charged and sentenced to years in prison because of things that they said! Their words caused them to be declared GUILTY!

When you stand before the King of kings and Lord of lords, will you stand accused or acquitted?

# UNCAP YOUR LIFE
## YOU SHALL HAVE WHAT YOU SAY!

**UNCAP YOUR LIFE**
**YOU SHALL HAVE WHAT YOU SAY!**

# Shhhhhhh!!
## 1 Thessalonians 4:11

*And that ye study to be quiet, and to do your own business,*
*and to work with your own hands, as we commanded you*

In this scripture, study means to "determine" or "aspire." in other words make a determination to "shut your lips," you don't always have to have a response or opinion.

Just because you are knowledgeable in an area or on a subject does not mean that everyone wants to hear what you have to say about it! This is a lesson that I had to learn. I figured, "hey, I know it so let me tell them!" One day it back fired on me because I gave the wrong information to someone, which caused the person to have to redo the work they had just done all because "I just knew what I was talking about."

I heard someone in a movie ( I can't remember which one ) say, "Mind your business man just mind your business!" if you focus on what you should be doing and accomplishing, you just might keep yourself from sticking your foot in your own mouth (like I did)!

One definition of study is: to look at closely in order to observe or read.
Before you speak make sure you understand the ramifications behind your words!

Have you ever been guilty of speaking on something without having all the facts just to find out that you were WRONG? Talk about mud on your face! The going back to apologize is the humbling part.

That is why it is imperative that you "study to be quiet!" literally make a conscious effort not to jump into everybody else's business unless you are asked!

It's almost like what I've heard people tell their back talking children, "don't speak until you are spoken to!" sometimes you have to sit back and wait on someone to ask for your opinion!

Speaking out of turn not only can "cap" your life, it can "cap" the lives of others. Telling someone that they can "never" accomplish a certain task or telling yourself that it looks too hard so there is no use in trying is putting a "cap" on your potential!

Far too many children have stopped "reaching for the sky" because some adult told them about their own hard luck story. They tried and failed and they pass that same mindset on to their children not realizing that they stymied the growth of that child's dreams!

Maybe someone has stymied your dreams asking you why you are starting a business or applying for a job that they think you are not qualified for!

I'm telling you today, don't you dare stop reaching for those stars! Don't you dare stop climbing! When you feel like telling yourself you can't, DETERMINE TO BE QUIET!

GET TO WORK WITH YOUR OWN HANDS and accomplish what you set out to do!

If you have jumped into another person's business and caused them to stop pursuing their dreams, if you have dashed the hopes of your children through your defeating words, humble yourself and go apologize!

Study or aspire to be quiet, you just might learn a thing or three!

## UNCAP YOUR LIFE
## YOU SHALL HAVE WHAT YOU SAY!

# SEE WHAT IM SAYING?
## Hebrews 11:3

*Through faith we understand that the worlds were framed by the word of God, so that what is seen was not made out of things which are visible.*

I know in school that many of you were taught that the world was created by a BIG BANG or what scientists like to call "The Big Bang" theory. Unfortunately what you have learned IS NOT TRUE! The world was literally made by the SPOKEN WORD OF GOD. So I guess, you could say that God spoke and BANG the world was created!!

Go grab your bible and turn to Genesis chapter 1 where I will prove my point.

In Genesis chapter 1 starting with verse 1 we read, *in the beginning GOD CREATED the heaven and the earth. And the earth was without form, and void* (that means there was NOTHING THERE); *and darkness was upon the face of the deep. And the Spirit of God moved upon the face of the waters. AND GOD SAID, Let there be light: and there was light!*

Let's continue on this journey and see how many times God SAID and THERE WAS!

**Verse 6: And God SAID**
**Verse 9: And God SAID**
**Verse 11: And God SAID**
**Verse 14: And God SAID**
**Verse 20: And God SAID**

## Verse 24: And God SAID
## Verse 26: And God SAID

and finally Verse 27: SO GOD CREATED MAN in His Own Image, male and female created He them!

Looking back on our reference scripture Hebrew 11: 3, you can now determine that since God framed or created the world BY WHAT HE SAID, we as mankind; made in His image and likeness have that SAME CREATIVE POWER WITHIN US!

You can frame your world by the words that you speak. You PAINT THE PICTURE of your life by your words. In those seven God SAID verses, God said, AND THERE WAS! HE SPOKE WHAT HE WANTED TO SEE AND IT CAME INTO BEING! You have the POWER to do the same!

How many times have you said, "You see what I'm SAYING?" in other words, you were using your words to CREATE A PICTURE OR IMAGE in someone's mind. If you notice on Facebook or any social media site, people can make post that makes their lives seem Magical!
By you reading their words, you form a picture in your mind of what their lives are like, even if their words are deceitful, you still form a picture.

Words are so powerful! I encourage you to take your life's picture and "frame it" with positive affirmations.

Even if it seems like all hell is breaking loose in your life, even if your finances have hit rock bottom, even if your marriage is on the rocks or your job is in jeopardy, FRAME YOUR LIFE WITH WHAT YOU WANT TO SEE!

Think about it....a picture frame can either add value to a picture or decrease the value of a picture depending on the frame. The right frame can make a Kindergarteners drawing look like a MASTERPIECE! All the scribbles and odd shaped circles look like a Picasso if it's placed in an expensive frame. However, that same scribbled picture with the odd shaped circles can look just like what it is, a kindergartener drawing; if placed in a Dollar Store frame!

Even if your life is filled with scribbles and tears, odd shaped circles and fragmented squares, SPEAK LIFE INTO IT! SPEAK those things that be not as though they were! Remember, the end of Hebrews 11:3 says, *"so that the things which are seen were not made of things which do appear."* your life may "appear" to be in shambles however your words can cause a NEW LIFE to be created!

If you don't like what you see, put a different FRAME around your life!

## UNCAP YOUR LIFE
## YOU SHALL HAVE WHAT YOU SAY!

# RIPPLE EFFECT
## Ecclesiastes 10:20

***Curse not the King, no not in thy thought; and curse not the rich in thy bedchamber: for a bird of the air shall carry the voice, and that which hath wings shall <u>tell the matter.</u>***

Spoken words echo through the mountain tops. If you are a movie watcher like I am, I'm sure you've seen those scenes where someone cups their hands over their mouths and shouts out "Hello?" which is instantly followed by an echo declaring, "hello, hello, hello."
In the really funny movies or comedies the mountain will sometimes "holla back" with something totally opposite of what you said. That's the problem talking about people to other people causes, you whisper in secret in one person's ear and they run and tell the story to the person you were talking about!

Sometimes their words are an exact echo of what you said, but most times, like the mountains in the comedies, they are totally opposite. That is why it is important to watch what you speak.

What you think is spoken in secret between two "friends" can often be revealed to family members, co-workers, lovers and your boss, the very people you were "talking about."

My spiritual dad Bishop Dennis Gilbert always says ***"What takes a bone will carry a bone!"*** In other words, the person who will listen to gossip, like that bird of the air in our reference scripture; will also carry that same gossip to another!

Once gossip gets going it spreads like a wild fire and the ripple effects can be devastating! James chapter 3 verse 6 says, *"And the tongue is a fire a world of iniquity: so is the tongue among our members, that it defileth the whole body, and setteth on fire the course of nature; and it is set on fire of hell.*

When you use your mouth to gossip and slander you have in essence allowed hell to use you as a vessel. Using your mouth to speak against others could cost you dearly!

Talking about your boss to a co-worker could cost you your job! Now you have successfully **"capped"** your finances!

Talking about your cousin to another cousin could result in a family dispute, now you have successfully **"capped"** your family relationships. The ripple effect behind that is multiple families are involved as the mother and fathers argue, the siblings of the cousins argue and others in your family choose sides.

One little stone tossed in a pond causes ripples that extend throughout the pond. One misspoken word can cause a lifetime of regret. It's sad to say but some people love running to mischief, they get joy out of seeing strife and contention.

Be careful of whom you share your intimate thoughts with, even the good thoughts; because sharing them with the wrong person can cost you greatly.

If you have something against anyone, I encourage you to go to them in secret. Talk to them about whatever concerns you have about them, you just might win your "brother/sister, friend, co-worker, and husband/wife back!"

The only way to stop a ripple or to keep that "little birdie" from spreading your gossip is to not gossip at all!

*A brother offended (wronged) is harder to be won (is more unyielding) than a strong (fortified) city: and their contentions (disputes, arguments) are like the bars of a castle (arguments separate friends like a gate locked with bars).*
*Proverbs 18:19*

Don't allow your words to destroy your relationships. Before spreading gossip, put a "CAP" on your lips!

**UNCAP YOUR LIFE**
**YOU SHALL HAVE WHAT YOU SAY!**

# THE HEART-MOUTH-CONNECTION
## Luke 6:45

*A good man brings good things out of the good stored up in his heart, and an evil man brings evil things out of the evil stored up in his heart. For the mouth SPEAKS what the heart is full of. (NIV)*

*A good man out of the treasure of his heart bringeth forth that which is good; and an evil man out of the evil treasure of his heart bringeth forth that which is evil: fir of the abundance of the heart the MOUTH SPEAKETH! (KJV)*

I know you've heard the saying "what is in you will come out"...well let me confirm through the Word of God that the saying is true! There is a connection between what is in your heart and what you speak!

In the preceding verses, 43 and 44 we read where Jesus is discussing good fruit and bad fruit. He noted that in the natural a good or healthy tree doesn't produce rotten or corrupt fruit and on the flip side of that coin, a corrupt or diseased tree cannot produce good or healthy fruit.

He continues on to say that every tree is known by its fruit, in other words an apple tree is recognized or identified because of its apples; a pear tree is known or identified by its pears. It is impossible to go to an apple tree and get pears! That just doesn't happen because it goes against the very reproductive nature of the apple tree!

Jesus then starts speaking of mankind (which is actually what He's been addressing all along!) He was driving home the fact that what you see in a person is their very nature. It is what they are made of. When they speak, they are actually speaking from the heart!

The treasure of your heart or what you hold dear will always reveal itself through your speech!
Have you ever been talking to someone and even though they are speaking "happy" words, you discern that they are actually sad and broken. Why can you feel or discern that...because it comes from the heart.

No matter how hard you try, you can't hide for too long what is really in your heart.

If you are speaking negativity, it's because it's in your heart!
If you are speaking defeat, it's because it's in your heart!
If you are speaking hopelessness, it's because it's in your heart!

You are not going to see good fruit (or live a good life) by speaking negative words. If you are filled with doubt, unbelief, regret, heartache, heartbreak, bitterness, jealousy, etc... You will be known by that fruit!
It doesn't take long for people to see who you really are by what you say! Think about it, if a person is always talking about "needing" money or "needing" a hand up but never do anything to help themselves you

immediately begin to realize, by their fruit; that they are manipulators. It wasn't that they did anything, it's what they SAY!

If a person is always talking about how they have been hurt, used and betrayed but they never want to deal with that hurt and get healed, you soon begin to realize that sympathy and attention is what they are craving. They are speaking what is in them!

You might be asking, "How did my heart get filled with all this rottenness or negativity?"
Let's start at the beginning when your heart was pure and ready to be filled with greatness! The day you were conceived there was an all-out attack against your very existence! The enemy of our souls, who never wanted you to realize your purpose nor fulfill your destiny, came after you with a vengeance causing your mom or dad to speak:

     * "I never wanted to be pregnant!"
     * "I don't want a boy, I wanted a girl!"
     * "Now I'm left raising this baby by myself. I should just give it away
     * "I should have gotten an abortion!"

What if you had an amazing mom and dad who welcomed you, cared for you during pregnancy and raised you in a loving and safe environment, how could your heart be filled with negativity? Let's take a look at the first day of school. You headed off to school with great expectation just knowing in your heart that you were going to have an amazing day until you were confronted by other kids who called you stupid, fat, or ugly!

Maybe there was a boy or girl that you liked but they rejected you because you weren't one of the "cool" kids.

This is where the filling of your heart began. Those seeds were planted in you before you had a fighting chance! Your mind then began to rehearse those words over and over again until there was a "treasure" or abundance of negativity in your heart!
You have up until this point been watering those seeds and bearing the fruit thereof but today I need you to know that there is hope! That hope is in Jesus!

Today I encourage you to ask Him to create in you a clean heart (an empty slate) and renew a right spirit (one that is not damaged) within you. Ask Him for the Fruit of The

Spirit so that instead of negativity, you'll be filled with and bring forth **Love, Joy, Peace, Long suffering, Gentleness, Goodness, Faith, Meekness, Temperance.**

When your heart is filled with these things, your mouth will speak it and your life will show it!
The heart-mouth connection is a powerful one. FILL your heart with Love and take the "cap" off of your LIFE!

# UNCAP YOUR LIFE
## YOU SHALL HAVE WHAT YOU SAY!

**UNCAP YOUR LIFE**
**YOU SHALL HAVE WHAT YOU SAY!**

# LOVING LIFE AND GOOD DAYS
## 1 Peter 3:10

*For he that will love life, and see good days, let him refrain his tongue from evil, and his lips that they speak no guile:*

Before we discuss the "Four R's" I want to leave you with this. It is not only possible to have a good life; it's actually possible to have a life that you LOVE!
In previous sections, we discussed the consequences of speaking negative over your life; we will now talk about how to ensure good days and a life you love.

Notice that the scripture says, "Refrain the tongue from evil and the lips from speaking guile (deceit.) This is the secret, the answer to enjoying life!

**Life** is defined as: *the condition that distinguishes animals and plants from inorganic matter, including the capacity for* **growth, reproduction, functional activity, and continual change preceding death.**

By refraining from evil speaking such as grumbling, complaining, backbiting, slander, etc... And refusing to allow any deceitful thing to come out of your mouth; you open yourself up to good days!
Think about it, most people who grumble and complain are often without very many friends, why....because who wants to constantly spend time with someone who seems to only see the negative side of life! That gets tiring!

And if you are always talking about someone, you drive people away too because now it is assumed (and is probably true) that you talk about everybody! I know I don't tell my business to people who backbite and gossip! That's a news headline, inbox, tweet or text message waiting to happen!

Loving life means growing! It's time to put off immature and old ways of thinking. Your past is over, what happened or didn't happen to you is passed! There is a saying, "we live, we learn" it's time to learn from our experiences and change what we don't like by speaking what we do! Your words are seeds! Plant good ones and over time, you'll see the *growth* you've been desiring!

You *reproduce* what you speak, if you're always declaring your business will fold, it will.
If you keep speaking that your marriage will fail, it will.


Your words are *reproducing*; they plant, incubate and then bring forth whatsoever YOU are saying. Start saying "I can have, I will do, this will succeed" and you will see good days!

Know that this life is about *change*, nothing stays the same and that right there can be a great thing! The Greek word for transformation is *metamorphosis.* It is a *profound change in form from one stage to the next in the life history of an organism.*

We normally hear about metamorphosis when we talk about butterflies. As you know, a butterfly starts its life as a caterpillar; it then turns into a pupa (gets into its cocoon) and eventually and after some struggle; comes out as a beautiful butterfly. All this happened over the *life history* of the caterpillar, it didn't happen in one day!

I say that to encourage you, when you start speaking positive life filled words; change is not going to happen overnight. Just life the caterpillar you are going to face rough times, high moments and low, but eventually, if you keep your mouth from evil and your lips from speaking guile, YOU WILL LOVE LIFE AND SEE GOOD DAYS!

I trust that you will start thinking before you start speaking, remember, you can "Uncap" your life! Your new beginning is just around the corner!

**UNCAP YOUR LIFE**
**YOU SHALL HAVE WHAT YOU SAY!**

# THE FOUR R'S

Now that we have dealt with the power of your words and how your words can literally cause manifestation into your life, let's look at how we can correct those things that we spoke in ignorance (without knowledge.)

The four "R's" **Renounce, Repent, Reverse and Reinvent**; will help us put our lives back on the right tracks and cause our lives to flourish.

In this section I will define each word and guide you through how to put them in action. Your words got you into trouble, now your words will help get you out! Like the parent telling the child who is whining for attention, I tell you today....

## USE YOUR WORDS!
## (TO YOUR BENEFIT THAT IS)

To **Renounce** something according to *Webster's Revised Unabridged Dictionary* is to: formally declare ones abandonment of a claim, right, or possession. To regret or decline formally. It comes from the Greek words *Apotithemi* which means to put off or lay aside and *Apekduomai* which means to strip off from oneself.

If you really want to see change in and take the limits off of your life, renouncing your previous words or actions IN PRAYER will have to take place first! You have to give up any right or claim to have a bad attitude, seek revenge, to walk in self-pity, self-doubt, self-rejection, "self-centeredness", fear, insecurity, etc.... these things are normally the culprits behind the words you speak that "CAP" or put limitations on your life.

You have to literally regret the things that you said or the actions that you performed, lay them aside, strip them from your very being and determine within yourself that you will not pick them up or put them back on again NO MATTER WHAT!

**Renouncing** tells the spirit realm that you are no longer connected to, whether by bloodline or declaration; any negative confession concerning you! It stops the flow or negative manifestation and puts a "cap" on it!

After your renounce, strip off, abandon and lay aside your previous words and works, you have to repent.

To **Repent** from the Greek *meta* and *noieo* means to think differently or afterword's; to reconsider. It's to change one's mind for the better, heartily to amend with abhorrence of one's past sins.

This is where you "self-examine." you have to get introspective and find out why you feel the way you feel and why you do what you do. Many times self-defeating words are spoken due to ones outlook on the world, their lives or their surroundings.

You have to change your perspective (change your mind.) it's time to start thinking differently. You have to "hate" your current situation enough to do something about it! You can't keep doing the same thing, the same way and expect to get a different result, that's insane! It's time to **repent** and do better! It's time to make a change and reverse what you've been speaking!

To **<u>Reverse</u>** something is to go in the opposite direction or as the *Oxford Dictionary* defines it: to go in or turn toward the direction ***opposite*** to that previously stated. It's a complete change of direction.

To continue to speak in ways that will limit or stymie your life is just like setting a collision course to destruction! It's time to "**reverse** the curse" so to speak.

Remember, Life and Death is in the POWER of the tongue! What you speak into the atmosphere will manifest in your life whether good or bad. Life has already taught us, what goes in must come out, what goes up must come down; what is BROKEN needs to be fixed! It's time to put your life into **reverse**! Hit the gas pedal (use your words) and change directions!

For every NEGATIVE declaration spoken, **reverse** its effect on your life by speaking POSITIVE, LIFE AFFIRMING WORDS!

* "I can't" must be replaced with "I will!"

\* "Nothing good ever happens to me" must be replaced by "I will have good success!"

\* "I'll never be happy" must be replaced with "I will be happy all the days of my life!"

\* "I'll never get married" must be replaced with "I am worth the wait, he/she is on the way!"

\* "I'll always be broke" must be replaced with "Money is drawn to me like a magnet!"

You have to earnestly fight to reverse the curses you spoke over yourself! Take your life back! Go in the opposite direction! CHOOSE LIFE! CHOOSE BLESSING! CHOOSE INCREASE!

If you don't like the way your life is heading,
**PUT IT IN REVERSE!**

Last but most definitely not least, you have to
**Reinvent!**

To **Reinvent** is to change so much that it appears to be entirely new! To remake, make over, as in a different form.

You will actually be "Reinventing yourself!"

In Christ, old things are passed away, all things become new! You put on a new man; you're transformed by the renewing of your mind. Nothing about you remains the same.

I remember seeing a young lady I went to school with, honestly I didn't know for certain if it was her because she looked "different." I hesitantly called her name and she turned in response. I exclaimed, "It is you! Girl you lost so much weight I almost didn't recognize you!"

Her response, "I've been working on me!"

She had **reinvented** her life. She no longer struggled with diabetes, sleep apnea, high blood pressure or joint pain; why... because she had become a "new man." she now enjoyed dating (she hadn't before), she enjoyed shopping when at first it only frustrated her; she was actually enjoying life now because she had a new outlook!

She had done a complete makeover! She didn't look like the woman I used to know, she had changed so much that she appeared to be an entirely new person! That my friend is **reinventing** yourself!

It's time for you to do the same thing! No more up and down life, no more hard luck stories, and no more woe is me pity parties! Get up, dust yourself off and **reinvent** your life!

It's time to put those Four "R's" together! Pray this prayer of renouncing, repenting, reversing, and reinventing with me! It's time for you to LIVE!

Say, *Father in the Name of Jesus. I come to you acknowledging that I have caused a cap to be put on my own life. Many times I blamed you for my failures and even got mad at you but now I realize the truth; I spoke the life I'm living now into existence!*

*In the Name of Jesus, I* **renounce** *every word curse that I have spoken over my own life and every word curse I received from another. Forgive me for not guarding my lips and just allowing anything, in the heat of the moment; to come out of my mouth!*
*I* **repent** *of the way I view my life. I make a choice to change my mind, to wholeheartedly change the way I think about life, myself and others.*
*I bind and* **reverse** *every negative word spoken over my life and I loose your plans for me. Your Word tells me that your thoughts towards me are good and not of evil, to give me a hope and an expected end! I choose the life you have for me, not the one I created with my negative words!*
*And now Lord I ask that you* **reinvent** *me! Lord make me over! Take out my stony heart and give me a heart of flesh! Make me a new creation in You! For my life I cry out, "Not my will but Your will be done in me!"*
*Now Father, I thank you for my new life! I thank you for new ways of thinking and living! I thank you that new seeds of life are sprouting in my life and they are replacing the negative seed I once sowed! I thank you that my life will bring forth a HARVEST of good all the days of my life!*
*I thank you Lord that from this moment forward I AM NO LONGER THE SAME!*

*In times of trouble, help me to set a guard at my lips!*
*Help me remember to be slow to speak! Help me to*
*study or think about my words BEFORE I speak them.*
*Thank you Father for showing me how to take the CAP*
*OFF OF MY LIFE!*
*I AM FREE! I AM TRANSFORMED! I AM NEW!*
*In Jesus Name I decree IT IS SO!*
*Amen and Amen!*

Hallelujah to the Lamb! I am so excited for you and your new beginning! I know that if you prayed this prayer in faith the CAP has come off your life!

Begin to give God praise now for your breakthrough! Thank Him for your new beginning! The limits have been taken off of your life in Jesus Name!

****

Now that you've **renounced** your former words and actions, **repented** and changed your mind, **reversed** the curses over your life and have laid aside all that WEIGHT; it's time to start LIVING!

Walk into the newness of life and experience the peace you've been longing for all your life!

****

I pray that this guide or reference book has been a blessing to you. It is my desire to see the people of God walk into the very life and blessings that God has already ordained for us. The word of God says that He came that we might have LIFE and that MORE ABUNDANTLY and that's just the life I'm going to have! I hope you determine to have that life to its there waiting for you to reach out and grab it!

My last encouragement to you is this, the next time you are listening to a charismatic preacher or a cheer leading life coach PAY ATTENTION to what they ask you to repeat!

You just got through taking the CAP off of your life, DONT PUT IT BACK ON!

> ~~Written in LOVE,
> Apostle Octavia Standley

## OTHER TITLES BY OCTAVIA STANDLEY

## TALL, LIGHT AND HANDSOME
## FROM HURT TO HEALING

**If you are interested in booking
Apostle Octavia Standley for your next Conference,
Gathering or Seminar; please email all request to:**

**remnantministrieskc@gmail.com
or
pastorostandley@gmail.com**

**We look forward to hearing from you!**

**UNCAP YOUR LIFE
YOU SHALL HAVE WHAT YOU SAY!**

Made in the USA
Las Vegas, NV
05 June 2021